HIGHLIGHT... ENGLISH 2

Susan Duberley

HEINEMANN EDUCATIONAL

Heinemann Educational
a division of Heinemann Educational Books Ltd
Halley Court, Jordan Hill, Oxford OX2 8EJ
OXFORD LONDON EDINBURGH
MADRID ATHENS BOLOGNA PARIS
MELBOURNE SYDNEY AUCKLAND SINGAPORE TOKYO
IBADAN NAIROBI HARARE GABARONE
PORTSMOUTH NH (USA)

First published 1992
93 94 95 96 97 11 10 9 8 7 6 5 4 3 2

British Library Cataloguing in Publication Data for this
title is available from the British Library.

ISBN 0 435 10315 6

Designed and typeset by
Ian Foulis & Associates
Cover design by Green Door Ltd.
Cover photograph from Joy Myrdel
Text illustration by David Barnett and Sally Artz
Printed and bound in Hong Kong

Acknowledgements
The author and publishers would like to thank the following for permission to reproduce copyright material.

BBC Radio 5 for interview with Judy Simpson by Mark Curry from *On Your Mark*; BBC Radio 4 for extract 'Elsie and the Block of Ice' from *You and Yours*; BBC Magazines for 'The Amazing Radio 1 Chart Quiz' from *Fast Forward*, August 1-7 1990; Samantha Bedser for 'A Letter to a Friend' by Samantha Bedser from *Selected Poems from the Observer National Poetry Competition,* Observer/Puffin; *Big Magazine* for article 'Neil Patrick Harris'; Faber & Faber Ltd for 'Dusk' by Judith Nicholls from *What on Earth* by Judith Nicholls; *Hampstead & Highgate Express* for article 'Bully for the players who reveal the truth' by Sue Norris, 28/9/90; IPC Magazines Ltd for 'Talking Advertisement' from *New Scientist* 4/11/89; James Clark & Co Ltd for extract from *The Night of the Scorpions* by Anthony Horowitz; Robin Klein for 'Hey, Danny' from *Win Some, Lose Some*, ed. Jo Goodman, William Collins Ltd; Methuen (incorporating Eyre & Spottiswood) for extract from *The Painted Leopard* by Peter Greaves, Eyre & Spottiswood Ltd 1982; Michael Rosen for 'Hot Food' from *Poems Selected by Michael Rosen*, Kingfisher Books Ltd 1985. Routledge for 'Starlings' by Lucy Hosegood from *Those First Affections*, ed Timothy Rogers; Studio Cinema, Coleford, Gloucestershire for Ansaphone message; D C Thomson & Co Ltd for 'Starscene' from *Jackie*, 2/3/91; Trentham Books/Neti-Neti Theatre Company for extract from *Only Playing, Miss* by Penny Casdagli; *Western Daily Press* for article, 'Talking Vacuum Comes Clean' *Western Daily Press* April 26 1989 and for article 'A Pop Record by Stars Bros...' and for article 'Town Centre English Lesson', 4/7/89; Whipsnade Wild Animal Park for Ansaphone message.

We would also like to thank the following for permission to reproduce photographs on the pages noted:

Index Catalogue Shop Ltd, p 17; Ingrid Pollard/Neti-Neti p 37; Phillip Parkhouse p 8; Rex Features Ltd p 20.

Contents

Unit 1 Food for Thought

HOT FOOD

We sit down to eat
and the potato's a bit hot
so I only put a little bit on my fork
and I blow
whooph whooph
until it's cool
just cool
then into the mouth
nice.
And there's my brother
he's doing the same
whooph whooph
into the mouth
nice.
There's my mum
she's doing the same
whooph whooph
into the mouth
nice.

But my dad.
My dad.
What does he do?
He stuffs a great big
chunk of potato
into his mouth.
Then
that really does it.
His eyes pop out
he flaps his hands
he blows, he puffs, he yells
he bobs his head up and down
he spits bits of potato
all over his plate
and he turns to us and he says,
"Watch out everybody -
the potato's very hot."

by Michael Rosen

ACTIVITY 1: with a partner

Listen to the tape of the poem a few times as a class.
With a partner, take it in turns to read the poem to each other.

ACTIVITY 2: as a class or in a group

Discuss the points below.

1 What is happening in the poem?
2 "I only put a little bit on my fork"
  Who is the "I" in the poem? How can you tell?
3 The poet uses the sort of words you or I use when we talk to each other. Pick out examples.
4 Is the poem funny? Does it make you laugh? Why?
5 Have you ever eaten anything too hot? How well do you think the poet describes what it is like to eat something too hot?
6 Do you like the poem? Give reasons for your answer.

ACTIVITY 3: with a partner or in a group

Discuss some foods that are difficult to eat.
Choose 4 or 5 foods.
Think about what could happen as you eat the food.
Write it down on a copy of the chart below.
The chart has been started for you.

FOOD	WHAT TO DO TO AVOID PROBLEMS	DETAILS OF WHAT MIGHT HAPPEN AND WHAT SOMEONE MIGHT DO
Jelly	Take small spoonfuls. Eat slowly and carefully	Jelly wobbles off spoon. Splat! onto Nan's best tablecloth. Tracey goes red, bites her lips, hopes no one has seen. Tries to pick jelly from tablecloth but it sticks. Pushes jelly onto the spoon with her fingers. Messy! There is a red stain where it has been. Covers it with her bowl.

ACTIVITY 4: on your own or with a partner

Write your own poem about eating something that can cause problems.
Pick the food you want to write your poem about.
Use some of the ideas from your chart to help.
Remember to use everyday words as if you were talking.

You could plan your poem by following the pattern of Michael Rosen's poem e.g. Michael Rosen begins by describing how different people eat potato.

The people eating the food carefully

We sit down to eat
and the potato's a bit hot — the food
so I only put a little bit on my fork
and I blow
whooph whooph
until it's cool
just cool
then into the mouth
nice.

being careful with the food

And there's my brother
he's doing the same
whooph whooph
into the mouth
nice.
There's my mum
she's doing the same
whooph whooph
into the mouth
nice.

the person who is not careful — But my dad.
My dad.
What does he do?
He stuffs a great big
chunk of potato
into his mouth.
Then
that really does it.

what happens when he or she is not careful

His eyes pop out
he flaps his hands
he blows, he puffs, he yells
he bobs his head up and down
he spits bits of potato
all over his plate
and he turns to us and he says.
"Watch out everybody -
the potato's very hot." — the warning given to everyone

ACTIVITY 5: as a class or in a group

Read the words in the bubbles below and discuss, or check up on, the meanings of those you are not sure about.

Some of the words are foods e.g. crisps.
Some of the words describe the foods e.g. crunchy crisps or soggy crisps.
Words that describe an object are called adjectives.
As you can see, the adjective you choose can tell you a lot about an object e.g. which sort of crisps do you like best, crunchy or soggy?

Read the words in the bubbles again.
Match the foods with a suitable adjective.
The first one has been done for you: soggy sprouts

Add some more adjectives of your own e.g. soggy, squelchy, squishy sprouts
Pick the ones you like best and use these to decorate your display of poems.

ACTIVITY 6: as a class or in groups

Play the food clue-card game. (Teacher's Pack)

UNIT 2 Speak up

Talking vacuum comes clean...

After the talking car...now meet the world's first talking vacuum cleaner.

When there is a problem with the vacuum, it plays a few notes of music and then gives a bossy order. It never says 'please'.

Some of the orders it gives are: "Hose is clogged — find out where it is blocked up." "Bag is full," or "Bag is not correctly fitted."

The new Hoover Audio System 300 was given its first public outing yesterday at the Savoy Hotel, London.

And the £170 vacuum knows when it can't put everything right. When something goes badly wrong it gives out the order: "Motor problem, call your Hoover shop."

ACTIVITY 1: on your own or with a partner

Read the article about the "Talking vacuum" and then answer the questions below.

1 What is the full name of the vacuum?
2 How much does it cost?
3 From what you read in the article, write down four things that can go wrong with a vacuum.
4 When the motor on the vacuum goes wrong, the vacuum tells you to call the Hoover shop. Why do you think the vacuum doesn't say, "mend the motor"?
5 Look again at the things that the vacuum "says". Write down some of the reasons why a talking vacuum might be quite helpful.

ACTIVITY 2: in a group or with a partner

Discuss all the things in the house that could "talk".
For each, write down some of the things they could say e.g.

Hot-water bottle "This water is too hot — put in some cold water."
"There is a hole in the bottle — buy a new one." etc.

Now do the same for other things that could talk e.g.
Push Chair "A wheel is coming loose."
"The brake is not on properly." etc.

ACTIVITY 3: on your own or with a partner

Read the article about talking advertisements below.
Then write down the missing words in the sentences in the box.

Talking Advertisement

As the pages of the magazine open, a voice speaks 42 words of advertising in 15 seconds.

The speech is like the voice you hear with toys that talk. The voice sounds more like a Dalek than a man or woman's voice; but you can hear each word clearly.

The talking advertisement can be made for as little as $4.

Adapted from New Scientist

A talking advertisement lasts for __ **A** __ seconds only. There are __ **B**__ words for each advertisement. The voice of the person in the advertisement sounds a little bit like the voice of a __ **C**__. You can hear each word very __ **D**

ACTIVITY 4: with a partner or in a group

You are going to make a talking advertisement for a magazine or comic.

- Pick one of the things that you discussed in Activity 2.
- Give it a name and a price
- Decide who would buy this item.

Use the details in the box in Activity 3 for **1** – **3** below.

1 Decide what you want to say in the advertisement. Remember that what you write must make people want to buy your item.
2 Now write the words for the advertisement.
3 Practise reading your advertisement in 15 seconds and like a robot.

Make tapes of the talking advertisements in your class.

ACTIVITY 5: on your own or with a partner

Read the notes on the pages below.
The notes are to help Megan give a 2-minute talk about litter.
The notes remind Megan:

a what she is going to say and
b the order in which to say it.

Now read the words in the speech bubbles **A** – **H**.
These show what Megan said during her talk, but the order has been muddled.
For each of the speech bubbles, work out where she is in her talk.
Match each speech bubble with the notes e.g. **F** = 5B

1. Show photo of beach.
2. Describe litter in
   a) Station Road
   b) Cinema
3. Litter is
   a) ugly
   b) Dangerous (Phil on beach)
4. All of us to blame
   a) Me (wrapper)
   b) Dad (packet)
5. How to help
   a) Make poster
   b) Make badges
   c) Help each other
6. End – describe Station Road without litter.

A

B

C

D

E

F

G

H

ACTIVITY 6: with a partner

You are going to help each other to give a 2-minute talk.
Decide what each of you would like to talk about e.g. something you feel strongly about, or something that really interests you.

Work out what you want to say.
Then make notes to help you remember what you are going to say (like the notes on page 10).
Put your notes on to card and number the pages carefully.

ACTIVITY 7: in a group or as a class

Work out some of the tips that you think might be helpful in giving a talk.
Make a list of the tips e.g. look at the person or people you are talking to.

ACTIVITY 8: with a partner

Practise giving your talk to your partner.
Take it in turns to listen to each other.
Use the list of tips from Activity 7 to help you. (There are further tips in the Teacher's Pack.)
Add any extra tips as you work together.

UNIT 3 Hot under the Collar

ACTIVITY 1: as a class, in a group or with a partner

Listen to and follow the story, *Hey Danny!* by Robin Klein.

"How could you lose such a big schoolbag?!" Danny's mother demanded crossly. "Dunno," said Danny. "I was sort of swinging it around by the handles coming home over the footbridge. Then it sort of flew out of my hands and fell down on to a truck whizzing along the freeway."

"And of course you forgot to write your name and 'phone number in it as I told you to," said Mrs Hillery. "Well then, young man, you needn't expect me to buy you another one. You can just save up for a new one out of your pocket money. In the meantime you can use that overnight bag in the hall cupboard."

Danny went to the hall cupboard and looked.

"Strewth!" he said. The bag was not just blue; it was a bright clear electric blue; like a flash of lightning. His last school bag was brown, inside and out, and it didn't show marks if your can of cola leaked or you left your uneaten sandwiches there for a month.

"Hey, Mum," said Danny. "I can't take this thing to school! Not something this colour. Can't I just bung my books and stuff in a plastic bag?"

"You certainly can't! It's your own fault for being so careless, and I don't want to hear one more word about it!"

The next day at the bus stop everyone stared at the blue bag and smirked.

"Hey Danny," said Jeff, who was supposed to be his mate. "That looks like one of those bags girls take to ballet classes."

"Aw, belt up, can't you," said Danny.

In the bus, the stirring went on and on as more people arrived. The trip to school only took twenty minutes when you had an ordinary brown bag; but with a dirty great hunk of sky to carry around with you, it took forever.

"It goes with his lovely blue eyes," said one boy.

"Maybe he's got a little blue trike with training wheels to match," said another.

They called him 'Little Boy Blue' until he got off the bus. He made a dash for his classroom and pushed the bag under his desk. Miss Reynolds was marking the roll when she looked along the row of chairs and saw the bag.

"That's a very smart bag you have there, Danny," she said.

"He's leaving home to join the navy," said someone.

"He's got a little blue sailor suit," said someone else.

At morning break Danny went into the art room and got some tubes of paint. He mixed the colours into a shade of rich chocolate brown and smeared it over his bag with his hankie. When the bell rang to go back to class he had a rich chocolate brown hankie but the bag was still clear blue. "Darn thing!" Danny muttered. "Nothing sticks to it."

"Just what are you doing in the art room, Daniel Hillery?" asked Miss Reynolds. "And what's that awful mess?"

"I was just putting paint on my bag," said Danny.

"You boys are NOT to paint things all over your good school bags. Clean up that mess and get to class."

But Danny told her he was feeling sick and could he please lie down in the sick bay for a while. He took his blue bag in there with him. He found the key to the first aid box for school trips and looked inside for something that would make bright blue bags brown. There was a bottle of medicine. Danny tipped the whole lot on to cotton wool and rubbed it into the blue bag. It didn't stick. But it did stick to his hands and the bench top.

"Danny Hillery!" said Mr Ferguson at the door.

"You know very well that no one is allowed to unlock the first aid box. What do you think you're doing?"

"Sorry," said Danny. "Just looking for an aspirin. The lid just sort of fell off this bottle."

"I think you'd better sit out in the fresh air if you feel sick," Mr Ferguson said. "And who does that odd looking blue bag belong to?"

"It belongs to the sports shed, Mr Ferguson," Danny said. "It's got tapes and stuff in it. Blue's our house colour."

He went and sat outside with the bag pushed under the seat and looked at it in despair. His class came out on their way to the sports field. They all grinned at him and at the bag as they went by. Miss Reynolds told him briskly to stop mooning about and to come along for sports.

On the way to the sports field Danny sloshed the bag up and down in a puddle of mud, but the blue only became shinier. He rubbed it with handfuls of lush wet grass from under the sprinkler but that just added more gloss to the shine. At the field he tossed his blue bag in among the brown ones, and it stood out like a lagoon among rocks.

"Hey, Danny, you having tap dancing lessons?" someone called out.

"Hey, Danny, where did you get that lovely knitting bag? I want to get one for my mum."

"Hey, Danny, where's your little blue bunny pyjamas?"

"Hey, Danny..."

Danny had had enough.

"That bag's very special, if you want to know," he said.

"Yeah, sure," everyone scoffed. "What's so special about it?"

"I had to beg my mum to let me bring it to school," said Danny. "It took some doing, I can tell you. Usually she won't let it out of the house."

He grabbed up the bag and wiped off any traces of paint and medicine and mud and grass stains. A lot of it had seeped inside through the seams and zipper. It would take some explaining when his mum saw it. There was her name inside, E. Hillery, in big neat letters. E for Enid.

"E. Hillery," said Danny, showing all the kids around him. "That bag belonged to... Well, if you really want to know, it went on the expedition that first climbed Mount Everest."

Everyone jeered.

"It did so," said Danny. "See, Sir Edmund Hillary, there's his name printed right inside. And that's why it's this funny colour. So it wouldn't get lost in the snow. It was in this very bag that Sir Edmund Hillary carried the flag they stuck on the top of Mount Everest."

Everyone went very quiet.

"Are you related to Sir Edmund Hillary?" Mark said.

Danny nodded modestly.

"Hey, Danny, can I carry that bag on the bus?"
"Hey, Danny, can I carry it back from the sports field?"
"Hey, Danny, can I have a go with it on Monday morning?"
"I'll have to think about it," said Danny, but he was frantically doing sums in his head. One dollar pocket money a week, school bags cost twenty dollars. With a bit of luck he might just make it before someone checked up on the spelling of Hillary!

ACTIVITY 2: in a group or with a partner

Answer the questions below.

1 Why does Danny say at the end of the story that the bag belonged to Edmund Hillary?
2 How many times did Danny lie? Highlight the places where he lied on your photocopy. Discuss why he lied.
3 Discuss why you think the twenty-minute bus journey to school seemed to take "forever" when Danny had the blue bag?
4 What makes the bag so embarrassing?
5 The story is set in Australia.
Some of the words in the story are not used in Britain:

freeway marking the roll dollar

What words are used in Britain instead of these?

ACTIVITY 3: with a partner or in a small group

Look at the pictures **A** – **H** carefully and work out what has happened.
Decide which situations are the most embarrassing.
Put them in order of embarrassment.

A

B

ACTIVITY 4: with a partner

Write a short story where the main character is embarrassed about something. Pick one of the pictures or something that has happened to you. You could use the way Robin Klein has written her story to help you e.g.

- the main character is at home or about to go out
- something embarrassing happens
- everybody is teasing the main character
- how the main character gets out of the situation

In your story try to make your character's speech as real as possible. (Look at the way Robin Klein uses speech.)

UNIT 4 Messages

ACTIVITY 1: as a class or in a group

Listen to the tape of two messages left on an answerphone.
The messages are also written out below.
Discuss which of the messages are most helpful and why.
If you were the person who owned the answerphone, how well do these messages tell you what you need to know?

ACTIVITY 2: with a partner

The next two pages describe times when you might have to leave a message on an answerphone.
You are going to practise leaving messages on an answerphone.
Look at **A** on the next page.
Work together to plan what you would say if you had to leave the message.

Remember:

- Think about how you will talk to the different people e.g. will you talk to a friend in the same way as you talk to someone who is offering a job?
- You may want to make brief notes before "phoning".

When you are ready to leave a message, one person pretends to switch on the tape recorder and says:

> I am afraid we are out at the moment.
> Please give your name and phone number if needed.
> Leave your message after the pips.
> Pip pip (up to ten pips)

When the pips stop, the partner leaves a message.

Talk about the way your message came out.
Could it be better?
Try again if you want to leave a better message.
Now change places so that your partner leaves the message.

Now do the same for **B**, **C** and **D**.

A A best friend, who moved to a new town, is coming to stay with you.
They are coming by train with an older sister, tomorrow.
The person next door is meeting them outside the ticket office.
Leave details on their answerphone so that they will know how to recognise the person (shown on the right).
Add any other details.

B You have lost a watch; the picture of it is below.
You read an advertisement in the paper which says a watch has been found.
Ring to claim the watch.
What will you say to prove that it is your watch?

In your message give all the details you think are needed.
Do not give your address. Leave a real or made-up phone number.

C You are interested in the job below.

> **WANTED.** Someone to exercise two poodles Mon - Fri. ½ hour a day. Small payment. Must be fond of animals. Phone: 8324.

Decide what details the person will need.
A lot of people may apply for the job.
Decide how the person putting in the notice will choose who to pick.
Now leave the message that you think will get you the job.

D You bought a raffle ticket from Mrs Syed who runs the Oxfam shop in town. You get a message to say you have won but will you ring her to give details of where you live so that it can be delivered.
Use the map below to leave details of how to get to your cottage.

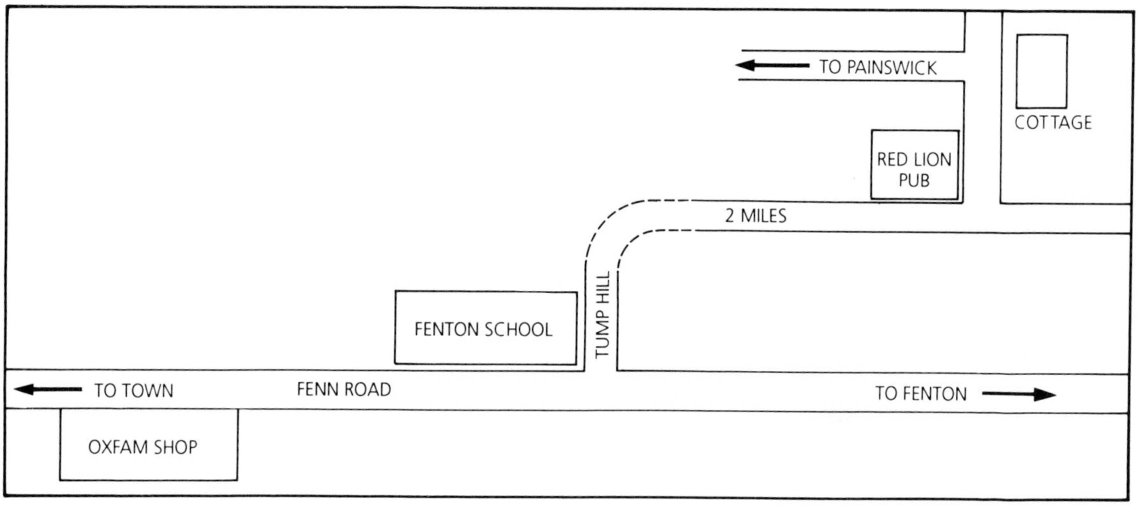

ACTIVITY 3: as a class or group

Listen to the taped message.
Jot down the answers to the questions below.
Find out how well you have remembered the message.

1 What time does *Three Men and a Little Lady* come on?
2 How old do you have to be before you can go to the film?
3 What is on in Studio 2?
4 How much will it cost if you go to this cinema?

Now do the same for the next taped message.

1 On what days of the year is the Wildlife Park closed?
2 How much does it cost an adult to go into the Wildlife Park?
3 What time does the Wildlife Park shut on Saturday in the Summer?
4 Who can you talk to at the Wildlife Park?

ACTIVITY 4: in groups of two or three

You are going to do the same as Activity 3, but for each other.
Your teacher will give each group a card with a message on it. (From the Teacher's Pack)
Check that you understand the message. Think of four questions about the message and write them down.

When everyone is ready:
one person in the group will read out the message,
one person will read out the questions,
the third person will give the answers.

Work out who will read the card, who will read the questions and who will give the answers.

Practise reading aloud so that you:
speak clearly
speak slowly
speak loud enough for everyone to hear what you say.

When everyone is ready, the first group comes to the front of the class.
They will read the card and ask the questions.
The rest of the class will jot down the answers.
One member of the group will give the answers.
The rest of the class check their answers to see how much they have remembered.

All the groups take it in turn to read, give the questions and the answers.

ACTIVITY 5: on your own or with a partner

Read **A** and **B** in the boxes below.
Choose ONE and write the message you need to leave.
Remember, you are not writing a letter, just a message or notes.

A

You are going on holiday for 10 days. You have a pet and have asked a friend next door to look after it. Write notes for your friend (aged 13), on how to look after the pet: e.g. food, bedding, etc.

B

You go out and leave a note on the kitchen table. Say when you went and give other details: e.g. where you have gone, who with, when you will be back, address or phone number, etc.

UNIT 5 Face to Face

NEIL PATRICK HARRIS

One of the best programmes on TV is *Doogie Howser M.D.*, the story of a whizz kid who's so brainy he becomes a hospital doctor at 15. We talked to the 18-year-old star of the show, Neil Patrick Harris, to find out what it's like working on the show.

It's lucky for us that Neil Patrick Harris became an actor because *Doogie Howser MD* wouldn't be the same without him.

Neil, who was born in Mexico, told us that he always knew he would be an entertainer, but he thought he would become known as a magician.

Magic is one of his favourite hobbies and he collects books and all sorts of new magic tricks. But he ended up in acting.

Neil said that more than 1,000 hopeful teenage boys tried for the role of Doogie, but he was the lucky one who got the part and he's still amazed at how popular the series is. "Yeah, I am surprised," he chuckles, as he chats to BIG at his home in New York.

"People come up to me and they are from Australia. They say how much they love the show. It's great!" But it's not an easy life being a star, Neil told us.

"Up until last year, I was doing a 10-hour day," he explains. "But now that I'm 18, they work me the full 12 hours. It's a hard day, but I can't complain — at least I am working. It's a real joy to be part of *Doogie Howser MD* and the scripts are wonderful."

So what is it like playing a doctor?

"Well, I don't feel like a real doctor would feel," he says. Still, playing a doctor has affected him he told us. He rushed to help a woman who had fainted in a shop and looked after her until a doctor arrived!

Adapted from Big Magazine

ACTIVITY 1: with a partner or on your own

Read the interview with Neil Harris.

Sometimes the reporter writes down the exact words Neil uses: e.g. line 18. Sometimes she reports what Neil says without using his exact words: e.g. lines 24/25.

Jot down the line numbers where the reporter:

a writes down the exact words Neil uses.
b reports what Neil says without using his exact words.

ACTIVITY 2: with a partner or on your own

Read what Neil says about the hours he works (lines 26–33).
Rewrite the same details but this time reporting what he says without using his exact words.

You might begin:

ACTIVITY 3: as a class, in a group or with a partner

Listen to the tape of the Radio 5 interview with Judy Simpson.
Discuss how much you can remember and make some notes.
Listen to the tape again, stopping sometimes to catch up on making notes.
Do not try to get everything down, just the general details.

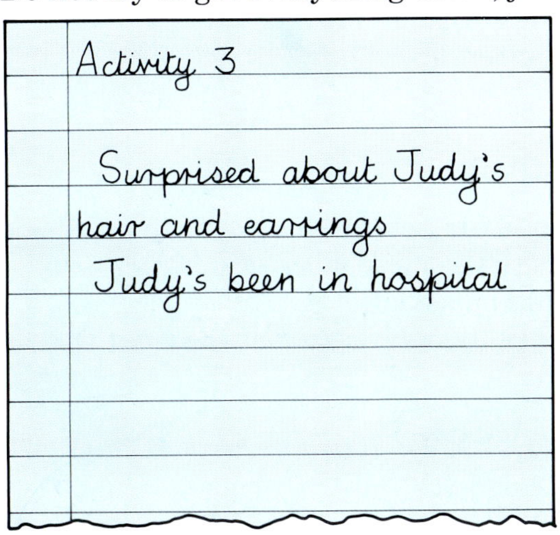

ACTIVITY 4: in a group, with a partner or on your own.

Imagine you were the reporter interviewing Judy Simpson.
Write up part of the interview or the whole interview with Judy Simpson.
Use the points below to help you.

- plan which details you will report: e.g. as you did in Activity 2.
- plan where you will use Judy's exact words.
- try to mix Judy's exact words and the reported details using the article on page 20 to help you.
- you may need to listen to parts of the tape again so that you can be sure of Judy's exact words.

Set out your final work to look as if it was in a magazine.

ACTIVITY 5: in a small group or with a partner

Look at picture **A** opposite.
Imagine that you are going to interview this person for Radio 5.
Think about some of the things that might have happened in that person's job.
Think about some of the people this person might meet and work with.
Work out the questions you could ask at the interview.

ACTIVITY 6: as a class or in a group

Listen to the questions each group has planned for Activity 5.
Discuss which questions you think would make the most interesting interview.
Discuss the order in which the questions could be asked.
Make sure that the first few questions are easy to answer so that they put the person at ease.

Now look at picture **B** and do the same as in Activity 5.

A

Mr Baxter

B

Jenny Peters

ACTIVITY 7: with a partner or on your own

Write a letter to one of the people in the pictures above.
Ask if they would come to your school to be interviewed.

- Work out the words you will use to invite the person to your school.
- Work out the details the person would need or like to know about your class and your work.
- Give details of the sort of questions you would like to ask. (Activities 5 and 6)
- Work out the words you will use to close the letter.
- Use the details below to help you set out your letter.

Draw and address the envelope in which the letter would be sent.

Highcroft School
Elm Lane
Hilton
Surrey
SR4 7SB

27-9-92

Dear Mr Baxter,

Yours sincerely,

Rakhi Sudera

UNIT 6 Ways of Seeing

ACTIVITY 1: as a class or in a group

Read the descriptions **1 – 8** below.
Now look at the pictures.
Each description can be matched with a picture e.g. 5 = G
"...the whole family lies on the grass like washing..."
This kind of description is called a simile.

Match the other descriptions with the pictures to make more similes.

Descriptions
1 like a loo brush (Robin Klein)
2 like bits of an umbrella (D.H. Lawrence)
3 falls like snow (Miho Tuan)
4 like a knitted blanket Nan once made (Kelly Smith, aged 11)
5 like washing (Ivor Cutler)
6 as an old, rough mat (Ted Hughes)
7 like small fat snakes on either hand (Francis Cornford)
8 like sausages (Michael Rosen)

G

H

ACTIVITY 2: as a class or in a group

A simile compares one thing with another e.g.

The boy had *hair* like a *loo brush*.

The description "like a loo brush" gives a picture of what the hair looked like.
Does this description help you to **see** what the hair looked like?
Read the rest of the similes from Activity 1.
Discuss which you think are the best descriptions.
Can you think of any other similes to describe the pictures in Activity 1?

ACTIVITY 3: as a class or in a group

Look at the pictures below and discuss some similes to describe them.
Think of a number of similes for each picture and discuss the merits of each.

A

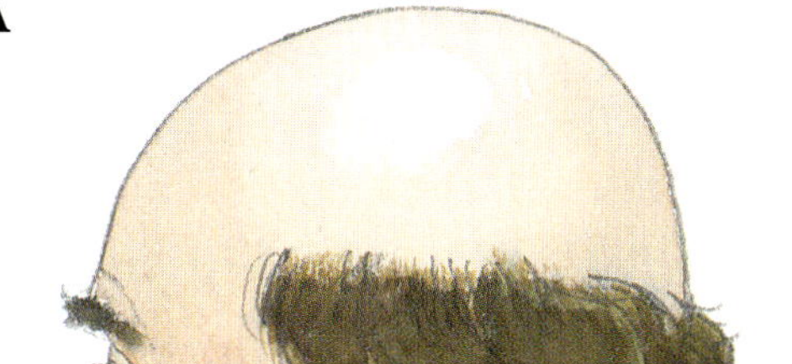

B

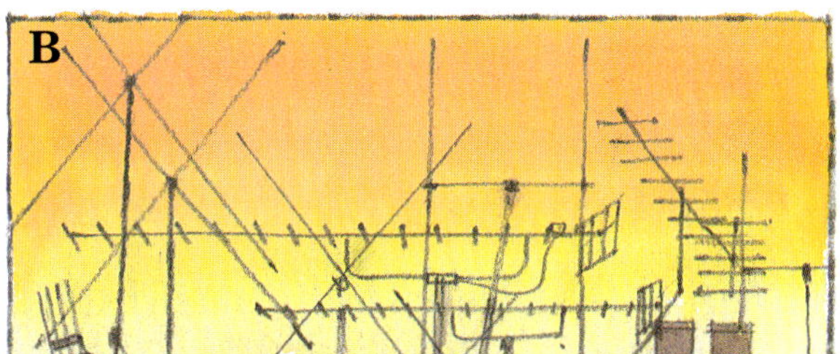

C

D

ACTIVITY 4: in a group or with a partner

Read **A**. Find the simile.
Does the simile help you to **see** what the butterfly looks like?
Are there any words in the poem that help you to understand more about the butterfly and how it moves?
Discuss whether you like the poem and why.

Read and discuss **B**, **C**, **D** and **E** in the same way.

A *Dusk* by Judith Nicholls

Butterfly, blinded
By smoke, drifts like torn paper
To the flames below.

B *Starlings* by Lucy Hosegood

This cold grey winter afternoon
The starlings
On the television aerial
Look like sultanas
On a stalk.

C *Timothy Winters* by Charles Causley

Timothy Winters comes to school,
With eyes as wide as a football-pool,
Ears like bombs and teeth like splinters,
A blitz of a boy, is Timothy Winters...

D And then... I saw a leopard standing upon a flattened rock, its spotted pelt gleaming and shining in the moonlight, so that it looked like a painted statue. A strange smell rather like musk, drifted to my nostrils.
The creature's eyes, beautiful as jewels, clear as spring water... wild and cruel as the earth itself, were fixed upon me.

Adapted from *The Painted Leopard* by Peter Greaves

E He (Dad) rang Doreen Slater up and she came straightaway, she had a horrible kid called Maxwell with her. It was quite a shock to see Doreen Slater for the first time...She is as thin as a stick insect ...She is just straight all the way up and down, including her nose, mouth and hair.

Adapted from *The Secret Diary of Adrian Mole aged 13¾*
by Sue Townsend

ACTIVITY 5: in a group or with a partner

Write your own short descriptions.
Include a simile in your writing.
Use ideas from the poems and descriptions in Activity 4 to help you.
Pick ideas to write about from what you see about you and where you live or write about two or three of the pictures below.

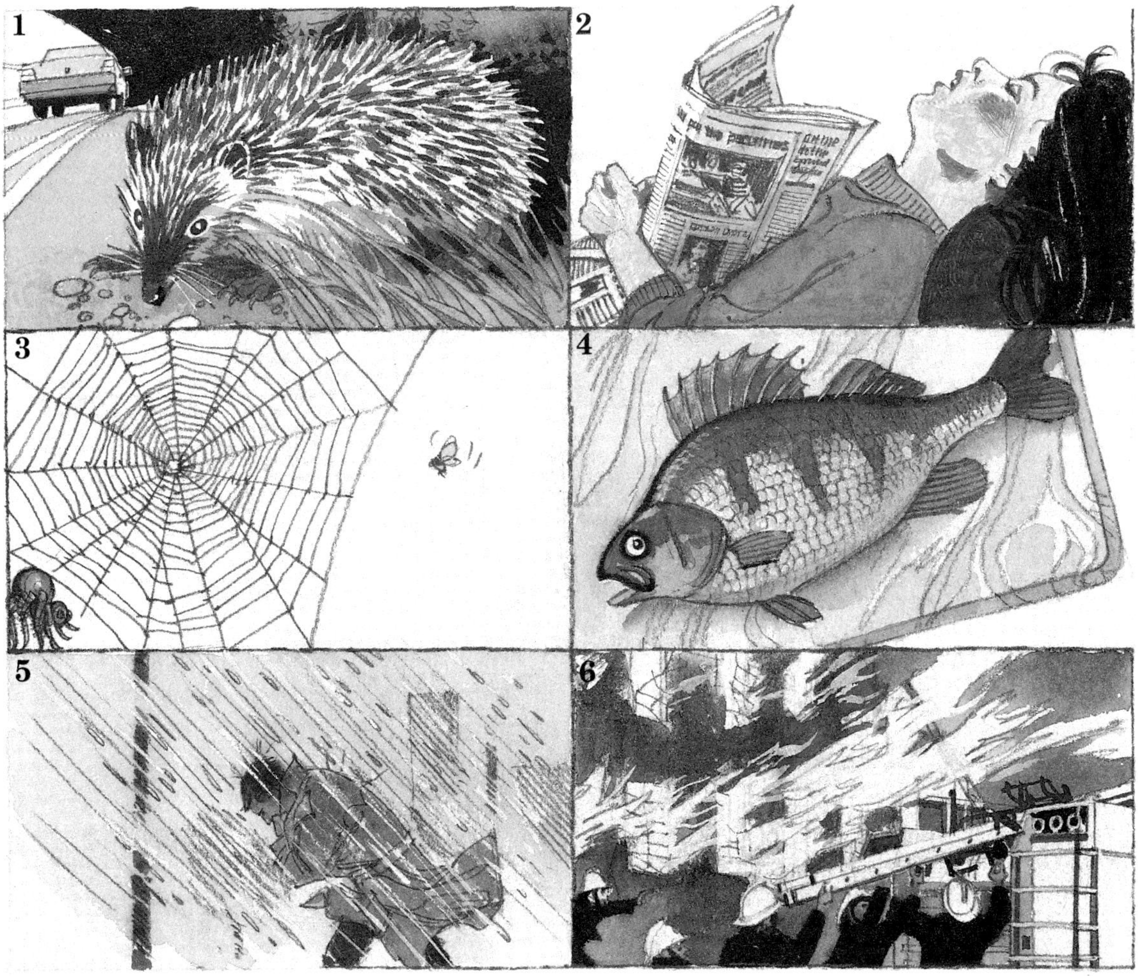

UNIT 7 Things to Come

Your Stars

ARIES
(21 March - 20 April)

FUN: Well, you won't have ANY fun if you start getting into a silly row. You've been warned!
LOVE: There may be some surprises in your love life this week.
MONEY: Try hard not to spend so much.

TAURUS
(April 21 - May 20)

FUN: You could be in for an overdose of fun this week ...you need a laugh.
LOVE: You are letting your love life get boring. Put a bit of zip into it.
MONEY: If you want money, you'll have to work for it. Sad, but true!

GEMINI
(May 21 - June 20)

FUN: You've got your head in the clouds this week. Be careful not to miss anything.
LOVE: Your love life could be good if you remember looks aren't everything.
MONEY: If you must borrow money, make sure you give it back as soon as possible.

CANCER
(June 21 - July 21)

FUN: Cheer up! OK. So you've been having a bad time lately, but stop moaning about it.
LOVE: Your love life will stay good if you put a bit of effort into it.
MONEY: You're not skint. So stop worrying.

LEO
(July 22 - Aug 21)

FUN: Make the most of this week. You are going to be very popular.
LOVE: Forget the past and move on. There may be a Tauran waiting for you.
MONEY: Be careful to check your change.

VIRGO
(Aug 22 - Sept 21)

FUN: Let your hair down this week. Have a crazy night out. You'll feel better.
LOVE: Your love life is not as bad as you think. You did open your big mouth a bit too soon, but it will come right if you wait.
MONEY: Get back the money that is owed to you.

LIBRA
(Sept 22 - Oct 21)

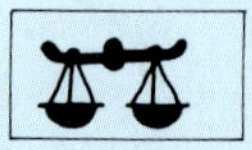

FUN: Your life should be buzzing this week; everyone will be asking you out.
LOVE: Two timing is not a good idea!
MONEY: You've saved some at last! Well done. Don't blow it all at once.

SCORPIO
(Oct 22 - Nov 21)

FUN: Stop moaning because you're not getting your own way. Enjoy yourself.
LOVE: It's time to forgive and forget. Stop sulking and things could look up.
MONEY: Watch where all your money goes.

SAGITTARIUS
(Nov 22 - Dec 21)

FUN: There could be problems at home. Give Mum a hand in the house.
LOVE: Your love life is looking up but it may not turn out as you expected.
MONEY: If you want any, start working!

CAPRICORN
(Dec 22 - Jan 19)

FUN: Listen carefully when you make plans this week. You could make a mistake.
LOVE: With your charm and wit, you could get the date you've been wanting.
MONEY: You're doing well, but save some.

AQUARIUS
(Jan 20 - Feb 18)

FUN: There should be heaps of fun this week when a Piscean comes your way.
LOVE: Keep trying. They will get the message soon. If they don't - who cares!
MONEY: Get started on your money making ideas.

PISCES
(Feb 19 - March 20)

FUN: Don't overwork yourself. If you try too hard you'll end up worn out.
LOVE: Your love life needs a bit of a lift, so try putting a bit of sparkle into it.
MONEY: A handy windfall could be on its way.

ACTIVITY 1: on your own

Answer the questions below.

1 Which is your star sign?
2 Which part of your horoscope do you like best? Why?
Which part do you not like? Why?
3 How many times are the words "could", "should" and "may" used on the horoscope page? Why do you think this is?
4 Write a sentence or two to explain the meaning of each of the sayings below. Use the pictures and the details in the horoscopes to help you.

to get the message
(Aquarius)

to let your hair down
(Virgo)

to open your big mouth
(Virgo)

to have your head in the clouds
(Gemini)

ACTIVITY 2: in a group of three or four

Read the **fun** section of the first horoscope: Aries.
Do you think that most people would like this part of the horoscope?
Give it a mark between 1 and 10.

10 is for a horoscope most people would like to have.
1 is for a horoscope most people would not like!

Go through the **fun** sections of all the horoscopes, agreeing a mark.
Then do the same for the **love** and **money** sections.

ACTIVITY 3: on your own or with a partner

Write the horoscope you would most like to have.

ACTIVITY 4: as a class or in a group

Read the paragraphs at the bottom of the page.
Discuss the questions below.

A What do you think is going to happen next?
B Why do you think this?
C What details do you expect to be in the next part of the story e.g.

what will the characters in the story say?
how will they speak?
what will they do?

Your teacher will give you the next three paragraphs.
Discuss each paragraph in the same way.

Martin pressed his finger against his eyes, trying to clear his head. When he removed them, a second later, the picture in his head returned. But now it was even more horrible.

The school was on fire. The flames blazed crimson behind the banks of black smoke that filled the classroom... All the desks were up-turned, with paper everywhere. He could see Robin West, lying with his eyes closed, a pool of blood forming around his head. Mr Reddy was standing with his back to the wall clutching his arm. There were people running everywhere, some of them beating at their burning clothes. One girl had plunged into a jagged hole that had opened in the floor. He could see the screams without hearing them.

Martin pushed his desk away from him and got to his feet, covering his eyes. "Yes, Hopkins?" Mr Reddy asked, stopping in mid-sentence. Martin looked up. The classroom was normal again. But he knew now, that it wouldn't be for long.

Adapted from *The Night of the Scorpion* by Anthony Horowitz

ACTIVITY 5: on your own or with a partner

Read paragraph five.
Continue the story after the accident. (One or two paragraphs)
Include in your story some of the details listed in Activity 4, **C** on page 30.

ACTIVITY 6: in a group of three or four

Below is a list of things that might happen in the future.
Decide which you think would be:

A Good. **B** Bad. **C** You need to know more or you cannot agree.

1 Everyone will earn the same money.
2 It will be impossible to tell a lie.
3 Families will only be allowed two children.
4 Smoking will be banned.
5 You will be able to read people's minds.
6 There will be no need to work.
7 There will be no need to eat food; you will only need pills.
8 You will be able to control the weather.
9 People will be able to choose the sex of their baby.
10 Children will not have to go to school if they do not want to.

UNIT 8 Buried in Time

A letter to a Friend (Not to be opened for 50 years)

Do you remember...
The time when we collected snails
And had snail races?
They left a silvery thread behind them.
Then we would stamp on them, shattering them.

Do you remember...
We used to collect up the grass
After it had been freshly cut,
Throwing it at each other
So that it fell down like confetti?

Do you remember...
When we used to make sandcastles,
Piling the sand in the buckets,
Tipping it out, forming the perfect mould,
A perfect pyramid of sand?

Do you remember...
When we used to do painting at play school?
We would both fight for the red paint;
I would always paint a red sun
Like a fat faced farmer smiling down.

I hope you will read this...
And remember the last threads of our
childhood.

Samantha Bedser, 13

ACTIVITY 1: with a partner

Read the poem a few times to yourself.
Take it in turns to read the poem to each other.
Help each other to get the feeling and the meaning of the poem over.
Make a tape of your reading.

ACTIVITY 2: on your own or with a partner

Make a sketch or picture for each of the descriptions (**A-D**) from the poem. **A** has been done for you.

A "...Sandcastles..
A perfect pyramid of sand..."

B "...we...had snail races?
They left a silvery thread behind them."

C "...grass ... freshly cut...
fell down like confetti..."

D "...a red sun
like a fat faced farmer smiling down."

ACTIVITY 3: on your own or with a partner

A Can you remember what you did when you were young?
Make a list of some of the things you shared with a friend — remember the happy times.

B Discuss your list with your partner. Pick 3 or 4 things you did that could be turned into a picture, as in Activity 2.

C Make a sketch for each of your "memory" pictures.

D Now write a few lines to describe each "memory" picture you have drawn.

ACTIVITY 4: on your own

You are now ready to write your own memory poem to a friend.
You could use the plan of Samantha's poem, below, to help you.

- Begin your first verse with the line: Do you remember...
- Lines 2 and 3 could say what you used to do e.g. When we used to build a den..., etc.
- Lines 4 and 5 could be the words you used to describe your first memory picture e.g. what the den looked like.
- Now do the same for the next two verses.
- Look at the last two lines of Samantha's poem. Then write an ending for your own poem.

ACTIVITY 5: on your own

You are going to make a life line, like the one below.

- Make a list of some of the most important times in your life, e.g. when you were born, when you acted in a play, when you had to go to hospital, etc.
- Add to your list other times that you will never forget, e.g. when you dropped the goldfish bowl, when you fell in the pond, etc.
- Work out what age you were when all of these things happened.

Now make your own life line, like the one below.

ACTIVITY 6: in groups of three or four

The picture below shows people in the year 2,500 opening a "Time Capsule". Discuss and decide on the answers to the questions below.

A What items would you put in a "Time Capsule" so that people in the future would know what it was like living now? Make a list.

B What would you put your items in?

C Where would you bury it?

D When do you think it would be best to open it? Say why you think this.

A pop record by stars Bros and a Neighbours video tape were buried yesterday.

The Bros record, the tape and a school dinner menu, together with packets of instant food, exercise books and a test tube containing dirty sea water, were among items placed in a time capsule by students at Woodroffe School, Lyme Regis.

The trunkful of items to show what life in the late 1980's was like, was buried and covered with a stone plaque.

Students from the first three years were asked to pick items for the time capsule.

"In 25 years time the same pupils will be asked back to dig it up again. They will be about 37 years old then," said Head of History, John Seabrook, who planned the project with another teacher, Ian Wood.

The trunk was buried near the school entrance by Tristan Harris and Natalie Price.

ACTIVITY 7: on your own; then as a group

Read the article above.
Write down the answers that the students from Woodroffe school would have given for **A** - **C** in Activity 6.

In a group discuss:
Do you think the pupils at Woodroffe School had better ideas than yours?
Give reasons for your answers.

ACTIVITY 8: on your own

Pretend your class has put together a time capsule and is going to bury it.
Write an article for your local newspaper like the one above.
Work out a headline for your article.
Set it out to look as much like a newspaper article as possible.

UNIT 9 Only Playing, Miss

Hampstead & Highgate Express, Camden FRIDAY, SEPTEMBER 28, 1990

Bully for the players who reveal the truth

The Neti-Neti Theatre Company explored the subject of bullying before writing *Only Playing, Miss*. Neti-Neti took the play around schools and later part of the play was shown on Thames Television's *Help*! programme and on the BBC *40 Minutes* spot. The result was a flood of letters from people of all ages, about bullying.

There is now a waiting list of 180 secondary schools which want to have the play performed.

Only Playing, Miss was written because Ms Casdagli was friends with an eight-year-old who was being bullied at school. "And I was bullied too," Ms Casdagli said. "Listening to my friend I remembered exactly how it felt."

Ms Casdagli is keen to see the end of all bullying. "School should be a safe place to go," she said. "In the play, Eugene is bullied because his father dies. He is punished for his unhappiness — and sadly this sort of thing happens only too often. Like everything else in the play, it is based on a real event."

The play, performed in English, British Sign Language and Bengali, is followed by anti-bullying workshops. "We can't deal with bullying forever, and we alone can't stop it, but we can try to help," Ms Casdagli said.

Sue Norris. Adapted

ACTIVITY 1: as a class or in a group

Read the article above then answer the questions.

1 Why did Ms Casdagli write a play about bullying?
2 Who is her play written for?
3 Why has Ms Casdagli written for this audience? What does she hope will be the result?
4 Where do you think Ms Casdagli and the other people involved, got the information they needed to write the play?
5 Why do you think the play is called *Only Playing, Miss?*
6 What do you think the headline means?

ACTIVITY 2: in groups of three

Read through the extract from the play by yourself.
Make sure you can understand all the words.
Then work out and discuss:

- what the characters are doing
- what the characters are like and how they are feeling
- how to read the lines so that what is said sounds real

Now each person takes a part.
Read the script making it sound as real as possible.
Remember to think about what is happening on stage.

SCENE 13: THE VALUE OF FRIENDSHIP

(EUGENE enters walking backwards, menaced by RANT. RANT grabs him by the arm and spins him round so fast EUGENE falls. He beats him up.)

RANT Come on, get up. Get up, mate, little Euge.

(He hits him on the side of the head.)

Hey, do you know what, I saw your Dad yesterday, at the bus stop. He looked so well.

(EUGENE jumps to his feet and grabs a chair. He holds it above his head as if he would throw it at RANT. RANT laughs.)

RANT Come on, throw it, Euge. Throw it!

(EUGENE lowers the chair and uses it as a shield against RANT. RANT kicks the chair.)

RANT What's all this? What's all this? Tough are you? Come on, lift it up. Do something, Eugene. Maybe you should tell your Dad about me. Get him to come and sort me out. Next time you see him, eh? See you later.

(He leaves. EUGENE lowers the chair, sits on it and puts his head on his hands. JO enters.)

JO You all right? What's the matter? What's up? Have they done it again? Have they? Who is it? Was it David? You've got to report him.

EUGENE I can't. I can't.

JO You've got to. Report him and he'll stop doing it.

EUGENE It'll only make it worse.

JO Have you told your Mum?

EUGENE She's got enough troubles of her own.

JO Tell her. It doesn't matter.

EUGENE Yes it does.

JO Look, you've got to do something. Every day they lay into you. Everyday they pick on you. You've got to do something. Why can't you?

EUGENE Because I don't want to.

JO Well you should. It'd stop.

ACTIVITY 3: as a class or in groups

Listen to the tape-recording of the script.
Read the script again using some of the ideas from the tape.
What did you change and why?

ACTIVITY 4: in a group

Listen to the tape again up until the next bleep.
Discuss what you think might happen next.
Listen to the rest of the scene and compare what you thought might happen with what actually happened.

Discuss the points below and back up your answers with evidence if possible.

- Is the language in the play right? Is this how people of your age talk?
- Do the characters seem real? Is this how people might behave?

ACTIVITY 5: in a group

Look at the photographs taken during the play. Discuss the questions below.

- What is happening in the photo?
- What might have been happening before the photo was taken?
- What might happen after the photo?

Pick one of the photos and write a scene or part of a scene for the play.
Work out the scene first using role play if possible.
Write your script using the points above and those in Activity 4.

If you have a second language, or English is not your first language or you use British Sign Language, include the language in the script.
In your final draft set out your play like the one from *Only Playing, Miss.*

ACTIVITY 6: in groups

Decide on, and write down in the form of a list, the tips and advice you could give a new student to the school to make sure they are not bullied.

Compare and discuss your list with the one students made in the Workshops that followed the play. (In the Teacher's Pack)

UNIT 10 Writing for Radio

ACTIVITY 1: as a class or in a group

Listen to the tape from *You and Yours,* Radio 4.
Stop the tape at the sound of the first set of pips.
Discuss the answers to question 1.
Listen to tape to check if you were right.
Carry on through the tape, stopping at each set of pips and discussing the question at that point.

1 What do you think Mrs Redford saw?
2 What do you think Mrs Redford thought might have happened?
3 What do you think she did?
4 Why do you think Mr Redford is so surprised?
5 What do you think Bob thought Mrs Redford should do next?
6 What do you think Mrs Redford was going to say next?
7 Can you think where the ice could have come from?
8 What would he do with the ice?
9 How did Dr Erberst explain the ice-ball?
10 What do you think he is going to say next?

ACTIVITY 2: as a class or in a group

You are going to make your own Radio 4 reports.
First you need to pick a subject for your reports.
Many strange things have been reported on radio, television and in newspapers.
Jot down some of the unusual things people have seen or say they have seen.

ACTIVITY 3: in a group of three or four

Choose one of the subjects you discussed in Activity 2.
Use the points below to help you work out the details for your report.

- Decide who saw what happened — person on paper round, shopkeeper, etc.
- Where were they at the time — in the house, in the park, etc?
- When did this happen — time of day or night?
- What did "it"/"they" look like — ghost, corn circle, etc?
- How did the person feel when they saw "it"/"them"?
- What happened next?
- Decide what another person, perhaps an expert thought about what had happened.

Now plan who will be the presenter, reporter and people interviewed.
Keep your report simple by having only one other person or expert involved.

ACTIVITY 4: in the same group as above

Look at the sort of details each person gives in the Radio 4 report below.

1. First sentence says what has happened and gets the listener interested

PRESENTER	Now we all know that Britain's weather can be a temperamental thing but even so you don't expect to get what looks like a huge hail stone weighing several pounds dropping on you, out of a clear summer sky. But that's exactly what happened to Mrs Elsie Redford and it transformed her from a Barnsley housewife to Elsie the Ice-maiden who has baffled scientists the length and breadth of her native Yorkshire. Jane Landen Davies has been hearing the details of her chilling tale.
JANE	Two weeks ago last Friday, an uninvited object came crashing into the life of Elsie Redford, a pensioner from Barnsley.
MRS REDFORD	It was about ten minutes to three. Well we were going out in evening and I thought, oh, I'll go and put some nail polish on. I'll go and get my nail polish. I just walked through here like, into this bathroom I...
JANE	On the Monday morning Elsie rang the Environmental Health Officer. He suggested the ice could have come from an ...
CAPTAIN MIMPRISS	The three sources are possibly from ...
PRESENTER	Well Elsie's experience is a rare one, but if it does happen to happen to you, you must ...

2. gives details about who saw what happened
3. introduces reporter
4. gives a bit more detail; introduces Mrs Redford
5. gives a lot of details
6. more detail; introduces expert
7. expert says what he thinks
8. ends report with what to do if it happens to you

Now plan what the people in your report will say and when they will say it.
You could write down fully what each person says, make notes or use role play.
Make a tape of your report for a programme like the one on the cassette.

ACTIVITY 5: with a partner

On the radio you hear all sorts of different items.
A - D on this page and the next are examples of four things you can hear.

A letter
B a joke
C part of a quiz
D a news item

- Read the letter.
- Make sure you can read all of the words; if not, ask for help.
- Why has Forhad written the letter? How is he feeling?
- Read the letter aloud.
- You will need to practise to get the feeling and the meaning of the letter over to the listener.

Work on **B**, **C** and **D** in the same way.
Two people can share the reading in **B** and **C**.
Watch out with **C**, you will need to read some parts very slowly.
Make a tape of your readings.

A

Dear Sir,
"Eid" is a big muslim festival and it is held once a year all around the world. I think it is very unfair to Muslims that when there is a festival like Christmas, we have lots of days off, but when "Eid" comes we don't have even one day off school. I think that the Muslims take the day off anyway, so that means we have to miss our lessons. I think something should be done about it.

Forhad Zaman
Birmingham

B

"Why are you crying little boy?"
"I was thirsty – sob! sob! – and I swapped my dog for a bottle of lemonade! Boo-hoo!"
"And now you wish you had him back, eh?"
"Yeeeessss! Waaaaaaa!"
"Because you realise how much you love him?"
"No – sob – cos I'm thirsty again!"

C

The Amazing Radio 1 Chart Quiz

BBC RADIO 1 97-99 FM

Well, waddya-know...here we go with... "The Amazing Radio One Chart Quiz." Yep siree, yet again, wonderful Radio 1 has done us proud and put together a package of the top ten selling singles.

And they're going to give them away! Yup. This week's top ten selling records could be yours if you answer these five questions and send the answers on a postcard to Chart Quiz 44, Fast Forward, PO Box 114, Leatherhead, Surrey, KT22 9DG.
1. Michael Jackson has three brothers and two sisters - true or false?
2. Radio 1's Jakki Brambles hates getting up early in the morning - true or false?...

D

A school went public yesterday.

Fifteen-year-olds sat at their desks for their Monday English lesson — in the middle of Dorchester High Street.

"People didn't seem to want to come and see us at work at school," Dr Melvin, the Headteacher said. "So we thought we would take our work to them."

Teachers will be giving lessons in the main shopping street, every day this week. So people will be able to see exactly what goes on in the classroom.

ACTIVITY 6: with a partner or in a group

Make a list of the sorts of things you would like to hear on a radio programme for people of your age.

ACTIVITY 7: with a partner or in a small group

Make a tape that lasts for about 3–5 minutes and that could be used on a radio programme for people of your age.
You could use your own ideas or those in **A-D** in Activity 5.
For example you could:

- pick favourite jokes and have a three minute joke spot.
- plan your own quiz on music, sport, wildlife, etc.
- write your own letters on subjects that you feel strongly about.
- write news items about things that are happening in your class/school.

Play your tapes to each other.

PUNCTUATION
Full stops and question marks

ACTIVITY 1: on your own

The story below has not been divided into sentences.
Read it and put in the capital letters and full stops.
Remember: do not begin a sentence with "and" or "but".

The boys waited at the bus stop it was beginning to get dark and there were no street lights on this road now it was getting cold as well the boys began to shiver the bus should have come by now perhaps they had missed it it was odd that there was no one else waiting

suddenly they saw a light coming up the road but it did not look like the lights of a bus they watched as the lights came nearer then they saw what it was coming towards them and started running away as fast they could

ACTIVITY 2: on your own

Read the paragraphs below.
Where there is a numbered star, put in a full stop or a question mark.

"We will be back at about eleven o'clock, " Mr Tomlin said. "Is there anything you want to know before we go **1***"
"Yes," Tessa said "What happens if he won't go to sleep **2*** Do you want us to sit with him **3***"
Mrs Tomlin smiled. "No **4***" she said. "He often stays awake **5***"
"Just look at all the food they have left us **6***" Tessa said when they had gone **7*** "Shall we eat it now **8*** I love those cakes **9***"
"You pig!" Jan said with a grin. "Do you come babysitting for the money or the food **10***"

There was a good horror film on the television **11*** Soon they were looking at a dark, damp cave **12*** Water was dripping on to a coffin in the corner **13*** Dracula was just about to open the lid **14*** Suddenly Jan sat up **15*** "Can you hear something **16*** " she whispered.
Tessa shook her head **17*** "What do you mean **18*** I can hear the telly."
"No," Jan said. "Listen. Can't you hear a dripping noise **19***"

Sentences

Two sentences can be joined e.g.

> The boy ran to the shop. The shop was closed.
>
> The boy ran to the shop but it was closed.

ACTIVITY 1: on your own or with a partner

Add one of the words from the box to sentence **1**.
Then finish the sentence e.g. sentence 1 could be:
The cat purred because I gave her some creamy milk.
Do the same with the rest of the sentences.

1 The cat purred ...
2 I might be able to come out ...
3 The girl laughed..
4 We will be late for school...
5 The headteacher smiled...
6 He put the money on the desk...

> when before
> if because
> where so

ACTIVITY 2: on your own or with a partner

Use the pictures and the words in the speech bubbles to write two sentences about each picture.
Join the two sentences with the words underneath the picture.

The first one has been done for you e.g.
A "I can come out when I have cleaned the kitchen floor."

Do the same for the other pictures.

A

when

B

because

C

but

D

until

Exclamation mark

An exclamation mark is used when a sentence is expressing strong feelings e.g.

3. capital letter
5. close speech marks

1. indent —— "How dare you speak to me like that!" Mrs Rolle shouted.

2. start speech marks
4. exclamation mark
6. full stop

ACTIVITY 1: with a partner or on your own

The stars in **1 — 6** below show where a punctuation mark has been left out.
Work out which sentences need an exclamation mark.
Write them down in your book, adding the exclamation mark.

1 "Sit down * " Keziah shouted.
2 "How are you * " Mrs Walsh asked, sweetly.
3 "Oh no * " Matt gasped. "I forgot to tell her * "
4 "I've lost the key * " Mrs Stevens sobbed.
5 "She's asleep * " Sapna whispered. "We'll ask her tomorrow *"
6 "I gave you two pounds yesterday * " Mr Dunn yelled. "You seem to think I'm made of money * "

ACTIVITY 2: with a partner or on your own

Work out the words that would go in the speech bubbles in **A** – **F**.
The words must express strong feelings and end in an exclamation mark.
Write the words down in the speech bubbles.

A

B

C

D

E

F

ACTIVITY 3: on your own

Using the words you planned in Activity 2, write a sentence for **A– F** above. e.g.
A could be: "Help me someone, I'm drowning!" screamed Sam.
Remember the points in the sentence at the top of this page.

Paragraphs

A paragraph is a sentence or a number of sentences about one idea.
Indent the first sentence of a paragraph.

ACTIVITY 1: on your own or with a partner

The boxes **A–D** show what happens when Donna is trying to cook a meal.
Write two sentences to describe what is happening in each picture.
The eight sentences will make a paragraph.
Remember to indent your first sentence e.g. for picture **A**:

Donna was looking forward to her supper. She stirred the scrambled eggs and kept an eye on the toast.

A **B** **C** **D**

ACTIVITY 2: on your own or with a partner.

You are going to write another paragraph about Donna.
Picture **E** shows what happened after Donna had burnt her supper.
Look at what happened when she went to the fish and chip shop.
Work out two things that Donna might have done before getting to the shop.
Write one or two sentences for each of your ideas.
Then write a sentence or two to describe picture **E**.
Work out what will happen next and write the last sentence of your paragraph.
Now write a third paragraph using picture **F** in the same way.

E **F**

Speech marks

Revision In a sentence when you write down the actual words people say, you put speech marks around them.

2. start speech marks 5. close speech marks 7. full stop

1. indent — "Don't tell her what I said," Rohan whispered.

3. capital letter 4. punctuation mark 6. capital letter

ACTIVITY 1: on your own

Read the words in the speech bubbles **A** – **C**.
Read the name of the person saying the words.
Write a sentence for each of the speech bubbles.

A **B** **C**

Tracey **Matthew** **Kim**

ACTIVITY 2: on your own or with a partner

To make writing interesting, you can split what someone is saying into two sentences, and add details in between:

"That's it!" Mrs Millar said, <u>switching off the television.</u> "Time for bed."

indent start speech marks close speech marks comma detail full stop start speech marks close speech marks

You are now going to do the same using the pictures on page 49.

Look at picture **A** and **a**.
Write down what Winston is doing while he is talking.
Now write two sentences for each of the speech bubbles, with your detail in the middle.

Do the same for the other pictures.
Remember the points at the bottom of page 48.

A

Winston

a

B

Mrs Morris

b

C

c

D

Marek

d

Revision Start a new line for each person, when two or more people are talking together.

"Do you want custard?" Mrs Potter asked.

new line ——— "No thanks," Dawn said.

ACTIVITY 3: on your own

Look at the speech bubbles and names in picture **A**.
Write a sentence for each of the speech bubbles.
Do the same for the other pictures.

Remember the point at the top of this page.

A

B

ACTIVITY 4: on your own or with a partner

To make writing interesting, you can use a split sentence (see page 48) for one of the people talking:

"I'm fed up!" Zak said, <u>slamming his book on the floor</u>, "I can't do those sums."

"I'll help you," Paul said.

new line detail

You are now going to do the same using the pictures on page 51.

Look at picture **A** and **a**.
Write down what Simon is doing while he is talking.
Now write two sentences for each of Simon's speech bubbles, with the detail in the middle.
On the next line, put in what Mr Webb says.
Do the same for the rest of the pictures.
Remember the points at the bottom of page 50.

Spelling - ar

ACTIVITY 1

Use the letters in the square below to make as many words as you can with "ar" in them, e.g. march.

n	f	b
d	ar	h
k	m	c

Good score: 16

ACTIVITY 2

Write down the missing word from the sentences below.
Each word must have the letters "art" in it.

1 Jenny loved _ _ _ _ _ _ _ _ _ a new book.

2 "There's a Top Ten _ _ _ _ _ in the music shop," Gordon said.

3 "You don't look very _ _ _ _ _ with your tie like that," Mrs Barca snapped. "Do it up properly."

4 "I got the main _ _ _ _ in the play, Mum!" Dynette shouted.

ACTIVITY 3

Write down the words for the pictures below.
Underline the word that appears in four of the words you have written.

Spelling - oa

ACTIVITY 1

Write down the words for **1 – 9** below.
Each word has "oa" in it.
Some of the words rhyme with each other.
Underline in the same colour each set of words which rhyme.
You should find three sets of rhymes.

1

2

3

4

5

6

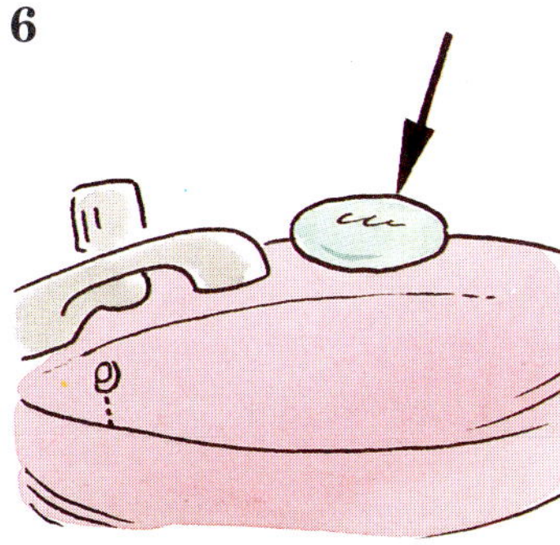

7

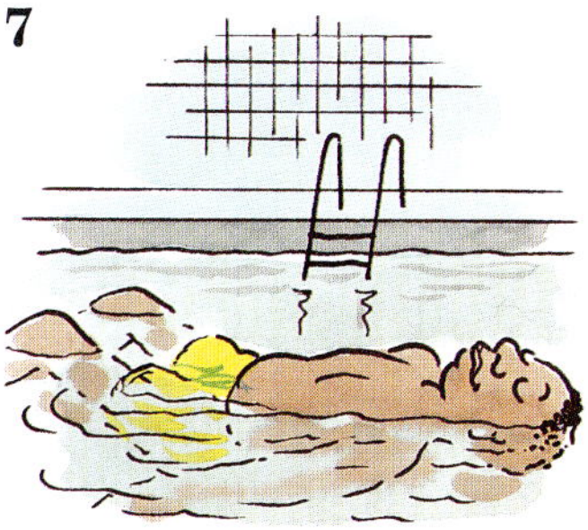

8

9

ACTIVITY 2

Write down the missing words from the sentences below.
Each word must have the letters "oa" in it.

1 You are always m _ _ _ ing and g _ _ _ _ _ _ _ _ about something. Cheer up!
2 "I got _ _ _ k _ _," Ghida said. "It's pouring with rain outside!"
3 "Get a _ _ _ _ of bread from the corner shop, dear," Mrs McCann said.
4 We sang all the way home on the c _ _ _ _ .
5 "The t _ _ _ _ is burning! Mr Smedley screamed "Turn off the grill!"

Spelling - ay

ACTIVITY 1

Write down the missing words from the sentences below.
Each word will have the letters "ay" in it.

1 "What did you _ _ _ ?" asked Craig.
2 The _ _ _ I like best is S_ _ _ _ _ _ .
3 They s _ _ _ _ _ in all day, because it was raining.
4 "If you hold the bat this _ _ _," Mrs Hall pointed out, "you will have better control."
5 "Were they still _ _ _ _ _ _ _ football when you left?" Lisa asked.
6 "My birthday is on the first of _ _ _ ," Amanda said loudly.

ACTIVITY 2

Write down the words for **1 — 3** below.
Each word ends with the letters "ay".

1

2

3

ACTIVITY 3

Use the letters below to make as many words as you can.
All the words must end in "ay".
Be careful, not all of the letters make words.
Some of the letters can be used together e.g.
1 stay

s	t	w		
p	l	r	b	ay
c	h			

Good score: 12 words

Spelling - or

ACTIVITY 1

Write down the words you can make ending in "orn" and "ort".
Put two words from each list into sentences.

b	orn	sp	ort
t		sh	
sc		s	
c		f	

ACTIVITY 2

Write down the words for the pictures below.
Each word must have the letters "or" in it.

ACTIVITY 3

Write a sentence for each of the pictures below.
Underline the word in each sentence that has the letters "or" in it.

Spelling - ai

ACTIVITY 1

Write down the words for the pictures below.
Each word has the letters "ai" in it.

1 2 3 4 5 6

ACTIVITY 2

Write down the words for the pictures below.
Put them into two columns, one ending in "n" and the other "l".

ACTIVITY 3

Fill in the missing letters below.

1 The big packet con _ _ _ _ s fifty rubber bands.
2 "This has gone bad," Mr Bakhsh com _ _ _ _ _ ed.
3 "Can you ex _ _ _ _ _ that again?" Jaswant asked.

Spelling - ou

ACTIVITY 1

Write down the words you can make ending in "ound".
Write one sentence using all of the words.
Use the picture to help.

p
gr
r
f
→ ound

ACTIVITY 2

Write down the missing word from the sentences below.
Each word must have the letters "ou" in it.

1 "Don't make a _ _ _ nd," whispered Ffion. "Mum's asleep."
2 "Open your _ _ _ th, please," the dentist said.
3 "Stop _ _ _ _ _ ing," Mr Pater snapped crossly. "Everyone will hear you a mile away!"
4 "You've every right to feel p _ _ _ _," Mr Cork said. "Not many people of your age can swim fifty lengths."
5 There was a _ _ _ _ noise and a crash and the next minute the cat came flying out of the kitchen.

ACTIVITY 3

Write down the words for **1** – **6** below.
Each word has "ou" in it.

1

2

3

4

5

6

Spelling - er

ACTIVITY 1

Use the letters below to make a list of words ending in "er".
Write two sentences using as many of the words from your list as you can.

clev

und

h

nev

farm

er

sist

temp

corn

ev

riv

ACTIVITY 2

You often add "er" to a describing word (an adjective; see page 7) if you are comparing one thing with another, e.g. Rikki is taller than Scott.

tall	taller	tallest

Note The letters "est" as in "tallest" show that you are comparing one thing with **all** of the others, e.g. Sasha is the tallest of them all.

Write down the missing words in the sentences below.
The words will end in "er" or "est".

1 "That's not fair!" Ann moaned. "My ice-cream is the small _ _ _ of the lot."
2 "It takes me long _ _ to get home than you," Aoife said.
3 "Is that the sharp _ _ _ knife you've got?" asked Nan. "I can't cut the meat with this."
4 "Can you talk a bit loud _ _ ?" Mr O'Dell asked. "I can't hear very well."
5 "Add some more sugar," Mrs Tan said. "It needs to be sweet _ _ ."

Spelling - oo

ACTIVITY 1

Write down the words for **1 – 7** below.
Each word has the letters "oo" in it.
Some of the words rhyme with each other.
Underline in the same colour each set of words which rhymes.
You should find two sets of rhymes.

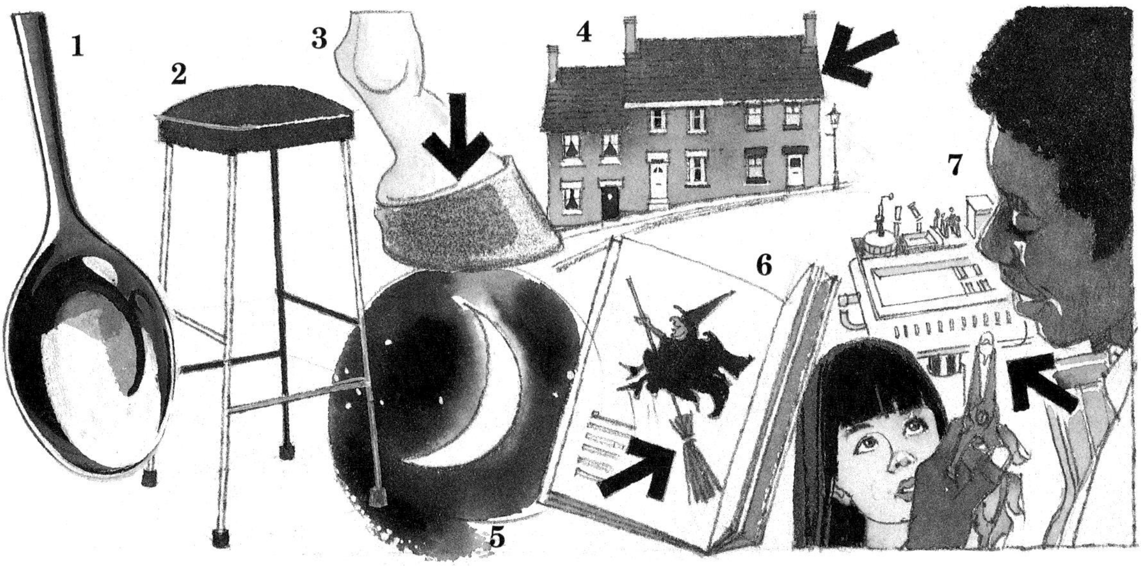

ACTIVITY 2

Use the letters below to make two lists of words, one with words ending in "oot" and the other list with words ending in "oop".
Write two sentences using some of the words in the first list.
Do the same using words in the second list.

sc

Sn

b

oot

h

tr

l

oop

dr

sh

sw

Spelling - igh

ACTIVITY 1

Write a sentence for each of the pictures below.
Use the word and picture to help with each sentence.
Underline the word in each sentence that has the letters "igh" in it.

fight

night

bright

fright

right

light

ACTIVITY 2

Write down the missing word in each sentence.
Each word will have the letters "igh" in it.

1 Mrs Jones yawned. "I'm so tired," she ____ ed.
2 "These shoes are too _____," Aruna said. "I need a new pair."
3 "How ____ are we making this wall, Dad?" Jade asked.
4 "The _____ of all that litter, makes me angry," Mr Simms shouted.
5 "Keep very still, and you _____ see the kestrel," Alun whispered.

ACTIVITY 3

Look at how you spell the word "height".
Write it down in large letters in your book.
Make the "e" of "height" a different colour.
Think of a way of remembering that there is an "e" in "height".
Write three sentences using the word "height".

Spelling - ea

ACTIVITY 1

Write down the words for **1 – 12** below.
Each word has the letters "ea" in it.
Some of the words rhyme with each other.
Underline in the same colour each set of words which rhymes.
You should find three sets of rhymes.

ACTIVITY 2

When "r" is added to "ea" the sound changes to "ear" as in "hear".
Write down the words you can make ending in "ear".
Write two sentences using as many of the words as you can.

d / t / y / f → ear

cl / g / n / h → ear

ACTIVITY 3

Look at how you spell the words on the right.
Write them in your book in large letters.
Make the word "ear" a different colour.
Then write a sentence using each word.

Spelling - ir

ACTIVITY 1

Write down the words for the pictures **1 – 7** below.

All of the words have the letters “ir” in them.
Some of the words rhyme with each other.
Underline in the same colour each set of words that rhymes.
You should find three sets of rhymes.

ACTIVITY 2

Write down the missing words in the sentences below.
All of the words will have the letters “ir” in them.

1 “I’ll give out the books, _ _ _ ,” Shakera said.
2 They all sang, “Happy _ _ _ _ _ _ _ _ _ to you.” Then Uncle Tom cut the cake.
3 “Wipe your feet!” Mr Batool shouted. “I don’t want _ _ _ _ on the floor.”
4 “You must be _ _ _ _ with your dogs,” the trainer said. “When you tell him to sit, say it as if you mean it.”

ACTIVITY 3

Copy the box below into your book.
Explain to your teacher how the “e” at the end of “fir” changes the word.

Then write down the words for the pictures below.
They end with the letters “ire”.

fir ⟶	fire

Spelling - ow

ACTIVITY 1

Use the letters in the square below to make as many words as you can with "ow" in them.
Make sure the "ow" sounds like the "ow" in "brown".
Some of the words will rhyme with each other.
Underline in the same colour each set of words that rhymes.
You should find three sets of rhymes.

l	c	b
n	ow	r
h	t	f

Good score: 12

ACTIVITY 2

Write down the words for **1** – **3** below.
All of the words have the letters "ow" in them.
All of the words end in "er".

1

2

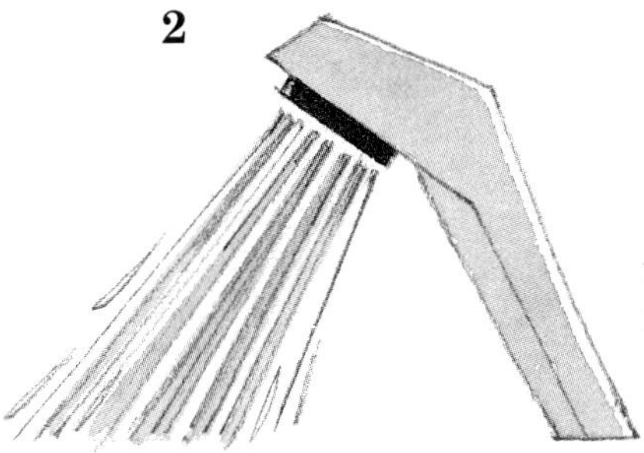

3

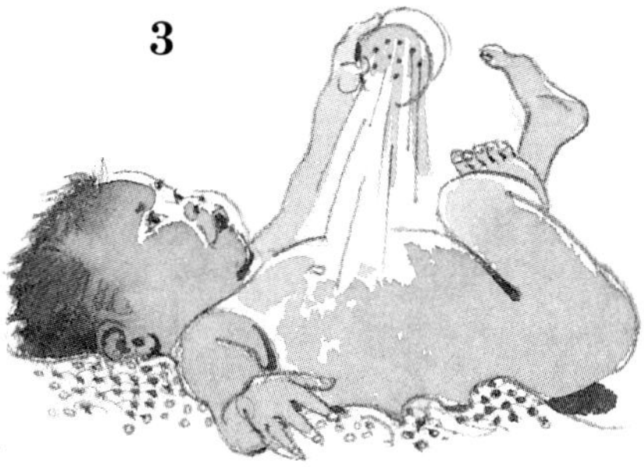

ACTIVITY 3

Write down the missing words in the sentences below.
All of the words have "ow" in them.

1 "The shops are always _ _ _ _ _ _ _ on Saturday," Helen moaned.
2 We went to Alton _ _ _ _ _ _ at the end of term.
3 "Lets put the box _ _ _ _ for a minute," Alia gasped. "I need a rest."
4 "Ben won't _ _ _ _ _ ," David said, picking up his sister. "Look! He's swimming back with the stick in his mouth."

ACTIVITY 4

Write down the words for **1** and **2**.
Both words have the letters "ow" in them.
Both of the words end in "el".

1

2

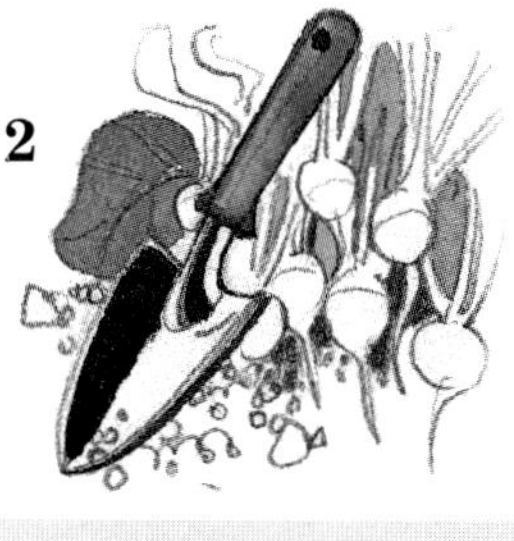